D1613601

SUPER SPORTS STAR

STEPHON MARBURY

Carol Plum-Ucci

Enslow Publishers, Inc.

40 Industrial Road	PO Box 38
Box 398	Aldershot
Berkeley Heights, NJ 07922	Hants GU12 6BP
USA	UK

http://www.enslow.com

Library of Congress Cataloging-in-Publication Data

Plum-Ucci, Carol, 1957–
   Super sports star Stephon Marbury/Carol Plum-Ucci.
     p. cm. – (Super sports star)
   Includes bibliographical references and index.
   Summary: Profiles basketball player Stephon Marbury, whose childhood dreams of an NBA career led him to play for Georgia Tech University, the Minnesota Timberwolves, the New Jersey Nets, and the Phoenix Suns.
   ISBN-10: 0-7660-1810-5
   1. Marbury, Stephon, 1977—Juvenile literature. 2. Basketball players—United States—Biography—Juvenile literature. [1. Marbury, Stephon, 1977– 2. Basketball players. 3. African Americans—Biography.] I. Title. II. Series.
GV884.M197 P56 2002
796.323'092—dc21   2001003255
[B]

ISBN-13: 978-0-7660-1810-5

Printed in the United States of America

10 9 8 7 6 5 4 3 2

To Our Readers: We have done our best to make sure that all Internet Addresses in this book were active and appropriate when we went to press. However, the author and publisher have no control over and assume no liability for the material available on those Internet sites or on other Web sites they may link to. Any comments or suggestions can be sent by e-mail to comments@enslow.com or to the address on the back cover.

Photo Credits: Andrew D. Bernstein/NBA Photos, pp. 13, 18; Nathaniel S. Butler/NBA Photos, p. 24; Chris Covatta/NBA Photos, p. 27; Jonathan Hayt/NBAE/Getty Images, p. 4; Glenn James/NBA Photos, pp. 22, 34; Fernando Medina/NBA Photos, pp. 11, 39; Robert Mora/NBA Photos, p. 36; NBA Photo, pp. 10, 41; David Sherman/NBA Photos, p. 20; Jon Soohoo/NBA Photos, p. 30; Kim Stallknecht/NBA Photos, p. 6; Catherine Steenkeste/NBAE/Getty Images, p. 45; Noren Trotman/NBA Photos, pp. 8, 15, 17, 28, 32.

Cover Photo: Catherine Steenkeste/NBAE/Getty Images.

CONTENTS

Introduction

Stephon Marbury plays the guard position for the Phoenix Suns of the National Basketball Association (NBA). When he first came to the NBA, he played for the Minnesota Timberwolves. After two seasons, he went to the New Jersey Nets. In the summer of 2001, Marbury was traded to Phoenix for Jason Kidd. Kidd went to the New Jersey Nets. Marbury calls plays on offense. He passes the ball to teammates so they can score. He sets the pace of the game. He also breaks up passes from the other team, steals the ball, and sets up scores.

Stephon Marbury is a hard-working, all-around player. He will do whatever it takes to help his team win.

Big Birthday Win

February 20, 2000, was a big day for Stephon Marbury of the NBA's New Jersey Nets. It was his twenty-third birthday. It was also the first time he would play against his old team, the Minnesota Timberwolves. The year before, Marbury had been a member of the Timberwolves. Now he was playing in New Jersey.

It was hard for Marbury to ignore 20,000 fans in Minnesota as they "welcomed" him onto the floor. Some fans screamed because they were happy to see him again. Some people booed. They wished he had not left Minnesota to play for the Nets.

Marbury had been a hero for the Timberwolves. He helped them get to their first-ever playoff game. He led the team in assists. In fact, of all the players in the NBA, he was the fourth best in total number of assists. Now, he had to play against his former teammates. He spotted Kevin Garnett, an old

Stephon Marbury plays well no matter what is going on around him.

friend, before tip-off. They hugged. Then the time to be nice was over.

Marbury plays well no matter what is going on around him. The score got close two times. Both times, he answered by slamming the ball through the net to score. In fact, he scored fourteen points in the first half.

In the second half, Marbury scored twenty-five more points. His former teammate Kevin Garnett was not playing well. He missed twenty-four of his thirty-three shots in the game—most in the second half. Terrell Brandon of the Timberwolves tried hard to stop Marbury from scoring. But Brandon fouled out of the game with four minutes left. Without Brandon to stop him, Marbury made another shot. The score was now 88–80 in favor of New Jersey.

Kevin Garnett got serious. He brought the score to 88–87. New Jersey was ahead by only one point.

When the game ended, the score was 91–89,

in favor of the Nets. The final score was a great birthday present for Stephon Marbury. "The best. It doesn't get any better than this," he said.

Not many NBA players score thirty-nine points during a single game. But Stephon Marbury is used to dealing with anything that comes his way on the court. He began building up his skills when he was just a young boy.

Stephon Marbury passes, steals, and sets up scores.

Growing Up

Stephon Marbury was born on February 20, 1977, in the Coney Island section of Brooklyn, New York. He has three older brothers, older twin sisters, and a younger brother. The apartment that he and his family lived in was not in a good neighborhood. Drugs and crime were all around. But everyone did their best to keep the basketball court safe. The court was called "The Garden." Players named it after Madison Square Garden. On that court, many kids, including Stephon Marbury, dreamed about someday playing in the NBA.

When Stephon Marbury was three years old, his big brothers looked like giants to him. Eric was twenty years old and was playing college basketball. Don and Norman were already high school basketball stars. Would pint-sized Stephon Marbury ever play basketball as well as his older brothers? Would he be better? Only time would tell.

Stephon's brothers were tall. They could dribble, pass, and shoot the ball well. Stephon's

When Stephon Marbury was a child, his older brothers would hold him up and say, "Shoot, kid!"

brothers decided to teach him how to play the game.

His brothers often took him to The Garden court. They held him up so he could reach the basket. They would say, "Shoot, kid!"

Crowds would watch. Stephon would shout out happily when he sunk the ball through the hoop. He wanted to make his brothers proud of him. Stephon dreamed of someday playing in the NBA. But he did not just dream. He also practiced. In fact, he kept improving every year. At age eight, he was good enough to play basketball with kids twice his age and size. Sometimes, he was even allowed to play in games with older kids at The Garden court. But most of the time, the bigger kids would not let him play. They said he was too young. That just made him work harder and dream about the NBA even more.

College coaches would visit The Garden to watch neighborhood high school players. They wanted to see if anyone might be good enough

Stephon Marbury shows his determination as he heads downcourt.

for their college teams. The coaches could not help but notice young Stephon Marbury. They often gave him free college T-shirts. By the time he was a sophomore in high school, he was getting more expensive things, like sneakers.

When Stephon graduated from high school in 1995, he was named All-America High School Boys Basketball Player of the Year. *Parade* magazine named him National High School Player of the Year. He was the top-rated high school point guard in the United States.

Many colleges offered Stephon Marbury scholarships. The schools would give him money to pay for his education if he would play basketball there. He said yes to Georgia Tech. He was excited to play for such a good team. He was also one step closer to making his NBA dreams come true.

A Year at Georgia Tech

Stephon Marbury started college at Georgia Tech in the fall of 1995. But things were not easy for him on the basketball court. After some games, he was not happy with the way he had played. His scoring and assist totals were good for a freshman. But he felt he should be playing even better. Near Christmas in 1995, Georgia Tech had a record of six wins and seven losses.

People started saying that Stephon Marbury might leave college early to enter the NBA. Coach Bobby Cremins told Marbury he was not ready for the NBA. "His assist ratio was poor, and he wasn't playing well," said Coach Cremins. But Marbury worked hard and became a better player.

Surrounded by defenders, Stephon Marbury goes up for the shot.

During a game against Georgetown University, Marbury played against Allen Iverson for the first time. Iverson was Georgetown's best player. Newspapers had been writing stories comparing Marbury and Iverson. Georgia Tech lost the game, 94–72. Still, newspapers were saying that Marbury had outplayed Iverson in the game.

Marbury made a promise during the game. "I was trying to do everything. From now on, I'm going to play my normal game. I'm not going to always look for the pass. I'm not playing like Stephon."

During his first year of college, Marbury averaged 18.9 points and 4.5 assists. With 679 points, he was the first freshman since Mark Price in the 1982–83 season to lead Georgia Tech in scoring. He was also named Third Team All-America by the Associated Press.

Marbury started hearing that some NBA teams were ready to draft him after only one year of college. The draft is the way that teams

Stephon Marbury was excited about being traded to the Minnesota Timberwolves.

choose new players each year. He had to think hard about that. His parents, Don and Mabel Marbury, wanted him to get an education. His three older brothers had been great basketball players in college. But none had gone on to play in the NBA.

Marbury did not know what to do. If he got hurt playing college ball, he might never get to the NBA. He decided to enter the NBA draft and finish his education later. He wanted to be able to help his family with the money he made in the NBA.

The Milwaukee Bucks drafted Marbury in 1996. But they traded him right away to the Minnesota Timberwolves. He was excited about the trade. He had always looked up to Kevin Garnett of the Timberwolves. In fact, by the time the trade came, they had already spent a lot of time talking on the phone. Marbury called Garnett his "phone bud." Now, he and Garnett would play the game together. Stephon Marbury thought the hard times were over for him and his family.

An Injury and a Comeback

On November 1, 1996, Stephon Marbury strolled onto the court as a member of the Timberwolves. He heard the applause of the huge crowd for the first time. He was nineteen years old. He was about to play in his first game in the NBA. *You're one of the youngest players in history.* Many people had been reminding him just how young he was. But he tried not to think about that. He needed to concentrate on doing well in the game. He had been playing with older guys his whole life. But the Timberwolves were not only older, they were NBA players.

He kept reminding himself how lucky he was to be there. He felt on top of the world. But that feeling did not last long. After only five minutes on the court, he fell to the ground in terrible pain. He thought his ankle was broken. Team doctors helped him to the locker room. His ankle throbbed. He bit down hard, in pain. He had played for only five minutes. Would he spend a year on the bench?

Stephon Marbury tries to get past Michael Jordan.

He was relieved when he found out that his ankle was just sprained. But he had also hurt his upper thigh. For eight games, he had to sit on the bench and wait until he felt better. That, he said, was one of the hardest times of his life. To help pass the time, he thought about how great it would feel to play again.

Marbury played harder than ever before after his injury had healed. In one of the first games he played after his injury, the Timberwolves were down by sixteen points in the second half. Marbury scored twenty-five of his thirty-two points in that half. Minnesota went on to beat the Milwaukee Bucks, 107–101.

On December 12, 1997, Marbury had twenty-one points, ten assists, and five three-pointers against the Phoenix Suns. The next day he scored fourteen

★
★ **UP CLOSE**
★
★

A favorite basketball memory for Stephon Marbury is when he won a high school championship game in the last few seconds by making two foul shots.

points against the Cleveland Cavaliers. He scored thirty-three points and had eight assists against the Utah Jazz on December 23. These were the highest totals of his NBA career.

Stephon Marbury is not a selfish player. He can shoot from just about anywhere on the court. But he never worries about being the center of attention. In a game against the Suns, he hit four three-pointers in the opening minutes. Then he started passing the ball to everyone else on the team. He wanted the other players on the team to have a chance to score. "He can get shots for himself anytime, and he doesn't do it," Coach Phil "Flip" Saunders said. "He is a total team player."

Marbury was named NBA Rookie of the Month in January 1997. He was very happy with what he had done so far.

In January 1997, Stephon Marbury was named NBA Rookie of the Month.

Friend to Young People

Stephon Marbury enjoys doing things for young people. In New York City, his basketball day camp helps kids from all over the country improve their game. He has a four-day basketball school each year in the Pocono Mountains in New York.

He also helps many kids in his old neighborhood of Coney Island visit his house in Maryland. He has a big swimming party for everyone. Teachers choose which kids get to go. They must be doing well in school.

He hosts the Stephon Marbury Basketball Classic (SMBC) on Coney Island each summer. It honors the memory of high school friend and teammate Jason "Juice" Sowell. "The kids win seven-foot trophies and jackets, and big-time bragging rights," Marbury says.

In spring 2001, Marbury began helping kids whose families could not afford medicine. Every time he got an assist on the Nets home court, he gave $100 to a special fund. The money helps buy medicine for people who need it. "I come

Stephon Marbury likes to help kids from his old neighborhood.

from a neighborhood in Brooklyn where kids didn't have access to the medical care they needed," he said. "The Children's Health Fund is delivering that crucial

care to thousands of children in neighborhoods like mine. I'm happy to be supporting their important efforts."

Marbury also likes to raise money to help other people. He helps out with Zo's Summer Groove. It is a big party for kids given by Alonzo Mourning of the Miami Heat. He also helps with Challenge for the Children. It is hosted by the musical group *NSYNC.

CHAPTER

6

The Best He Can Be

There is one thing about Stephon Marbury that fans can always count on. He will always work hard to get what he wants. Miami head coach Pat Riley had this to say about Marbury:

> "There are about five [great] point guards in the game and Marbury is right there with them. From a talent standpoint, he's something special. I've seen him grow and change. His body has changed. He has become very strong. He's so quick and he can shoot it. He's an exceptional player."

Stephon Marbury always tries to be the best he can be, not just at basketball. He also wants to keep a promise he made to his mother when he left Georgia Tech. He wants to finish

Stephon Marbury leaps
between two defenders to
make the shot.

his college education. He also wants to become an NBA head coach someday.

Stephon Marbury hopes to open a community center in Coney Island, New York. It will give young people free help with schoolwork. It will also be a place for them to play. His dream of someday playing in the NBA has come true. Now he wants to help young people make their dreams come true.

New Jersey Nets

Stephon Marbury made a big promise to himself at age ten. He said he would make it to the NBA and buy a nice house for his mother someday. By 1997, he had only been playing in the NBA for one year. But he kept his promise to his mom. He bought her a house in Maryland. He also helped his brothers and sisters move into nicer neighborhoods in New York.

But he could not be there to spend time with his family. New York and Maryland are very far away from Minnesota. He also did not like the cold, snowy Minnesota winters.

He was very happy when he got the chance to play for the New Jersey Nets. In March 1999, after two seasons in Minnesota, he was traded with Chris Carr, Bill Curley, and Paul Grant to the New Jersey Nets.

As he started his first season with the Nets, he thought about something his sister had said. *There's a price on everything. Nothing is free.* Marbury saw a lot more of his family. But being a Net in 1999 was not easy. Teammates were hurt and could not play. Jayson Williams was getting better from surgery to a broken leg. Kerry Kittles had surgery on his knee. It was up to Stephon Marbury and young forward Keith Van Horn to try to win games. But Van Horn was not shooting well. So Marbury tried to win games all by himself. He scored thirty-nine points in the first game of the season. In fact, he led the Nets in scoring in ten of their first eleven games. But the team lost ten of those games. One player cannot do it all alone.

"Guys were kind of in a funk," Marbury said. All of the players on the Nets needed to figure out how to play together to win.

Marbury began passing the ball more. Soon, the Nets got on a winning streak that almost took them to the playoffs. Marbury had a great

In March 1999, Stephon Marbury was traded to the New Jersey Nets.

season. He was the thirteenth-best scorer in the NBA. He was seventh best in assists.

In 2000–2001, his second full year as a Net was better than he ever thought it could be. He was named to the 2001 NBA All-Star Team. "This is not something that I fantasized about or thought about," Marbury said. "I never in my wildest dreams thought I would be playing in the All-Star Game. Where I'm from, you just want to make the NBA."

During the game he scored twelve points. Included in those points was a game winning three-pointer. His team, the East, had been behind by twenty points in the fourth quarter. They won in the last few seconds, 111–110.

Marbury knows how to win. He helped his team win the All-Star Game, even though he was in pain. He had seriously hurt his pinky finger the week before the game. That happened just after he sprained the same ankle twice in December. Then he hurt his knee. He sat out four games waiting for his body to heal.

Stephon Marbury was named to the 2001 NBA All-Star Team. His team, the East, won in the last few seconds.

41

When he finally played in the All-Star Game, he was still in pain.

Two nights after the All-Star Game, he scored a career high fifty points against the Los Angeles Lakers. He scored two three-pointers to send the game into overtime. Overtime is extra time added to a game that ends in a tie score. Marbury had not only fifty points, but also twelve assists. That was only the second time in the last twenty-five years that an NBA player had that many points and assists. Michael Jordan first did it against Washington in December 1992.

Stephon Marbury thanks his family for helping him make it this far. His big sister Stephanie says, "What you are witnessing now from Stephon is the labor of much prayer and hard knocks. I leave you with this. Challenge yourself. Challenge yourself to love, work and play as though it is your last day here on earth."

In summer 2001, Stephon Marbury got news that would change his career. He had been traded to the Phoenix Suns. In return, Jason Kidd would come to New Jersey from Phoenix. In his five seasons in the NBA, Stephon Marbury's scoring average has improved each season.

The Suns had a tough 2001–2002 season. But for the first time in fourteen years, the Suns won their final game of the season. The team pulled together, and Stephon Marbury helped his team win.

CAREER STATISTICS

	NBA						
Year	Team	GP	FG%	REB	AST	PTS	AVG
1996–1997	Minnesota Timberwolves	67	.408	184	522	1,057	15.8
1997–1998	Minnesota Timberwolves	82	.415	230	704	1,450	17.7
1998–1999	Minnesota Timberwolves	18	.408	62	167	319	17.7
1998–1999	New Jersey Nets	31	.439	80	270	725	23.4
1999–2000	New Jersey Nets	74	.432	240	622	1,640	22.2
2000–2001	New Jersey Nets	67	.441	205	506	1,598	23.9
2001–2002	Phoenix Suns	81	.441	262	653	1,659	20.5
2002–2003	Phoenix Suns	81	.439	263	654	1,806	22.3
2003–2004	Phoenix Suns/NY Knicks	81	.431	263	719	1,639	20.2
2004–2005	New York Knicks	82	.462	248	668	1,781	21.7
2005–2006	New York Knicks	60	.451	175	382	977	11.5
Totals		725	.435	2,216	5,880	14,666	20.2

GP—Games Played REB—Rebounds PTS—Points
FG%—Field Goal Percentage AST—Assists AVG—Average Points Per Game

Where to Write:

Mr. Stephon Marbury
c/o New York Knicks
Madison Square Garden
Two Pennsylvania Plaza
New York, NY 10121-0091

WORDS TO KNOW

All-Stars—Players from all of the teams in the NBA who are voted best at their position on the court. Teams made up of the best players from the Eastern and Western Conferences play against each other.

assist—A pass to another player that leads to a score.

freshman—A first-year student in high school or college.

overtime—Extra time added to a game that ends in a tie score.

point guard—The player who sets up plays, passes the ball, and sets the running pace for the team.

rookie—A first-year player.

sophomore—A student in the second year of high school or college.

three-pointer—A shot made from outside a painted line very far from the basket. It counts as three points instead of two.

READING ABOUT

Books

Hareas, John. *Slam*. New York: Scholastic Trade, 2000.

Jordan, Michael. *Official NBA Encyclopedia*. New York: Doubleday, 2000.

Lloyd, Bryant. *Basketball: Pass, Shoot, and Dribble*. Vero Beach, Fla.: Rourke Book Company, Inc., 1997.

Walton, David and John Hareas. *Official NBA Register, 2000–2001: Every Player, Every Stat*. New York: Sporting News, Inc., 2000.

Internet Addresses

The Official Web Site of the NBA
   <http://www.nba.com/playerfile/stephon_marbury.html>

The Official Web Site of the New York Knicks
   <http://www.nba.com/knicks/>

INDEX